MEMOIRS OF A COACH-OPERATING MAN

The Story of Falconer and Watts, coach operators of Llanishen, Cardiff (1919 – 1982)

by Rob Falconer

Cover photograph

HDW 873N, Falconer and Watts' first new 11-metre coach, a Ford R1114 with a Plaxton Panorama Elite III 53-seater body, purchased in 1975

(photograph copyright Rob Falconer)

Rob Falconer was born in Cardiff, the capital of Wales, far too long ago for him to remember the actual date. At present, he is still alive, but he checks the Times obituary every morning to make sure. Having gained a degree in psychology from Cardiff University, he passed his first interview with flying colours, and joined the family coach business "for a while" (actually around nine years). A history of the company can be found on his website, www.robertfalconer.co.uk.

He later became a computer programmer, before he and his job parted company in 2001. He has since written a number of short stories, and won competitions with The Times, International Mensa (he is a member), and the South Wales Echo. He has had a number of poems published in various anthologies :

'Puzzling Poems to Drive You Crazy' (Oxford University Press, edited by Susie Gibbs)
'How to Survive School' (MacMillan, edited by David Harmer)
'Read Me Out Loud!' (Pan MacMillan, edited by Gaby Morgan)

He has also written for comedy shows on both BBC and ITV.

His first book, 'The Return of Inspector Pirat: His First Book' (yes, I know, but you'll understand when you've read the book), came about because he often couldn't sleep, and amused himself by thinking up puzzles, which he then put into print. So, blame insomnia. Many of the stories are based around locations he has visited, such as a gîte in the Loire, on which 'Truck Stop' is based (he has difficulty in sleeping abroad too).

His second book, 'Pirat's Early Cases' was published in paperback and Kindle versions in late April 2016.

A third Inspector Pirat book, 'The Trial of Inspector Pirat,' was published in paperback and Kindle versions in February 2017, followed by a fourth, 'The Rebirth of Inspector Pirat,' in October 2017.

A sampler of four Inspector Pirat stories is available free on Smashwords.

His interests include pétanque, the cinema (but not necessarily modern cinema), crosswords and problem-solving, history, and reading detective fiction. His favourite detective author is Edmund Crispin, some of whose puzzles are truly ingenious, but laced with plenty of (often literary) humour.

He lives in Llandough, in Penarth, South Wales.

First published (Paperback / Kindle) : February 2018

Edition 1.0 – February 2018

ISBN (paperback) : 978-1985262737

**Visit Rob's website :
www.robertfalconer.co.uk/**

For Graham and Audrey

with thanks

Index

In which we consider other Cardiff coach operators, mostly anonymously!

Chapter 8
In which we are forced out by developers – We move our base to Kimberley Terrace, Llanishen – We have to find new space for our coaches

Chapter 9
In which Falconer and Watts is sold

Preface

I am writing and publishing this slim tome as there seems to be a continued interest in both the early days of Llanishen village in Cardiff (especially as so few of the older members are no longer with us), and our coach company, Falconer and Watts, which operated there from 1919 until 1982, when it was sold to Warners Fairfax Tours of Tewkesbury.

Personally, I don't think I've done enough in my long life to justify an autobiography, unless one along the lines of George and Weedon Grossmith's great oeuvre.

But I did enjoy my childhood and early years in Llanishen village, and almost ten years of my life working for the family coach business there.

I feel my experiences there represent those of just about any small country coach business at that time, and thus might interest anybody with an enthusiasm for small rural coach operators.

I also feel that my memories of village life in a country suburb of Cardiff from the 1950s and later might be of interest, not least to those many followers of Facebook sites about old Cardiff; and, especially, Llanishen.

So I thought that perhaps some of these experiences ought to be put into print.

I had wondered whether to disguise the company under an assumed name, but, well, that seemed unnecessary. Any other operators, and perhaps a few individuals, might very well need to be assigned pseudonyms "to protect the innocent," but, well, I reckon our company can cope.

Oh, and the title is a reference to 'Memoirs of a Fox-Hunting Man' by Siegfried Sassoon, which I was forced to read in high school (and no, I'm most definitely not a supporter of fox-hunting).

Rob Falconer
Llandough
February 2018

Chapter 1

In which, through no fault of my own, I am born into a coach-operating family – Some descriptions of village life – Schooling – A vast mechanical playground – The dangers of falling out of trees – Life as a bus spotter

By the time I was born, Llanishen had long before progressed from a small country village (enlarged and enlivened by the arrival of the railway in 1871) into a suburb of Cardiff, the capital of Wales.

Suburb perhaps, but a leafy and sylvan one.

Llanishen had been encroached upon sometime between the wars, or perhaps after, by the construction of two vast council estates to the north and south, cementing the village fairly and squarely as part of Cardiff ...

... and yet, it still retained its semblance of village life.

I cannot claim any credit for being born, and certainly not for being born where I was.

At that time, the village consisted of a main road with sundry shops in it, a Norman church, a double-nave public house opposite, and a blacksmith's, known as Miss Cosslett's, and reputedly haunted.

The church is very picturesque (I was married there in 1985), and I believe it is not apocryphal that some American fell in love with it and insisted on coming all the way over from the States to be married there. For the children of the village, it was most notable for having a lych-gate. Whenever those attending a wedding wanted to leave, the gate became mysteriously locked, and could only be opened by the local children on payment of a shower of coins.

Across the road from it is the Church Inn, so called, it seems, so that local husbands could say to their wives that they were popping off to the Church, apparently for ecclesiastical, rather than libationary purposes. There were rumours of a Roman tunnel from the pub to the church, although for what reasons no-one knew, especially as the tunnel would probably, in Roman times, have led from nowhere to nowhere.

Next to the church was Miss Cosslett's, a fairly traditional Welsh longhouse, with what was once the blacksmithery at one end and living quarters at the other. I remember it as being whitewashed and very old, but that didn't stop it soon being pulled down and replaced with an anodyne row of five shops and a police station (we had never been burgled until the first month the police station was opened almost exactly opposite our house: maybe thieves felt it gave them a reference point).

In Heol Hir, on the other side of the church away from the pub, was the village school. When my aunt, who had lived in London for decades, saw it, she described it as a "cowshed." Indeed, because of the new housing estates to the north and south of the village, in the nineteen-sixties the local council decided that the area needed a new school. They built a huge complex of buildings, all apparently made solely of glass, on what was to become the village by-pass. Almost all the parents had thought that, as the fabric of the school was so modern and forward-looking, the teaching must be the same, and so had moved almost all their children to the new see-through school.

Only a handful of pupils had been left at the old school (in these modern cost-conscious days they would certainly have closed it down), and so these had had almost personal tuition. Almost all the pupils there did really well in the end-of-school exams.

The building itself was very old and had been built sometime well before 1900. It had only two class-rooms partitioned into three, and had thick walls made of huge stones, as if the builders thought they might be reasonably required to withstand some sort of military attack. Surrounding the school was a wall made of similar stone, fascinatingly chock-full of small ammonites. The playground surface consisted of gravel and small loose stones, so that my mother was forever picking bits of grit out of my bloodied knees.

The PE equipment, which mainly consisted of hula hoops, was kept in the old air-raid shelter, and the toilets had plumbing reputedly dating back to Jacobean times.

The first school-room you were educated in was very quaint. It had a tall ceiling with a sort of belfry at the top. We were assured by Miss Robins that a little fairy by the name of Fairy Bluebell lived up there. Every Friday, she would tell us that, if we were very *very* quiet, then Fairy Bluebell would appear and leave little bags of sweets for all of us. We were sometimes not too quiet, but the good fairy always looked kindly upon us, and, although we never actually saw her, there were always sweets for us on Friday. It was years before we realised that Miss Robins, the dear soul, was paying for them herself.

It was also my first introduction to milk. The milk, in little bottles of probably around a third of the size of normal pints, was delivered by the milkman in tantalisingly-clinking metal crates. The milk was always left in front of the roaring fire (yes, a real fire) for at least half the morning, in order to take the chill off it. I hated the stuff. My parents tried every means possible to get me to drink it, even to the extent of buying very expensive little straws, each with a strawberry flavour capsule inside to turn the milk into something resembling a milk shake. I still hated the stuff. After this initial setback, it wasn't until I was into my late twenties that I realised that I adored milk, but it had to be straight from the fridge, stone-cold. Anyway, in those days, I doubt the school possessed a fridge.

Then I moved into one partitioned half of the other classroom. The partition could be pulled back if there were any large-scale occasions taking place, and I actually took part in one of these (but only once, I seem to remember). This was a school play, the title and author long forgotten, by me at least. I played Beelzebub, and had to caper around dressed in red crepe paper (can one still buy crepe paper?), with a balloon tied to one end of a stick, this latter device being the sort of thing that Satan himself would have used to terrify any unbelievers.

I remember I particularly hated having make-up applied, even if this was by Miss Smith, whom all the dads fancied. Nevertheless, this was apparently part of the ritual of theatre.

But the school was old, and had clearly been built solely for educational purposes, an aspiration which would certainly not include putting on any sort of heretical drama. We had to enter stage left, from the first classroom, usually under a gentle push from Miss Smith, and then exit right, past the boilers (the hellish aspects of this clanking, wheezing area would have suited Beelzebub down to the ground). We then continued around the outside of the school back into the first classroom.

Which was perfect as long as it didn't rain.

Which, of course, it did.

At the start, the audience was treated to a splendid version of Beelzebub, resplendent in the bright red crepe paper. However, as the afternoon wore on, and the Devil was required to make frequent entrances and exits, his clothing became gradually more soggy and ragged, until it finally detached itself entirely from Satan's body to lie in a sad little pile near the air-raid shelter.

For the rest of the play, Beelzebub had to rely solely on his threatening use of the balloon-on-a-stick to instil any degree of menace into the audience.

I normally hated sports, and indeed was pleased when I was allowed to boycott playing on the blood-stained gravel to spend playtime cutting up, "scoring" (a new word for me), and then gluing bits of cardboard together to make pointless little models.

However, I did enjoy sports day. This was held annually in the grounds of the Vicarage (why such a modest house enjoyed such a large and extensive field adjoining it I never did find out). The sports themselves weren't of much interest, as I was rather out-of-condition, and never won anything ... but we had warm lemonade (presumably preparing us for the iniquities of warm beer in pubs) and sticky buns. However, even these failed to instil a love of sporting activities in me.

The only other thing I remember about the Vicar was that he managed to mess up the only outing we ever had in that school. We all went by train to Haverfordwest and then by bus to St. David's Cathedral. Such an expedition! We all half-expected to meet Mungo Park en route. The train journey was especially exciting for me as we were one of the few families who had access to a car (in fact a whole fleet of them, as that was part of the family business), and so we never travelled by train. But we had to share the carriage with the Vicar's daughter who had been included in the trip at the last moment. I remember thinking at the time that this would be a very good thing were the train to crash, as our carriage would no doubt be spectacularly saved by God, who always looked after his own people. However, He had singularly failed to provide her with the requisite lunch pack, so we all had to give something from our packs to her so that she had something to eat. That somehow took the edge off the whole day, especially as I thought she could at least have tried praying for something first.

The main shopping thoroughfare in Llanishen was Station Road, which led from the centre of the village all the way up the hill to Llanishen Station, about a mile away. The shops were a mixed bunch, and varied greatly over the years, so that residents are forever trying to remember the name of "that wool shop" or when such-and-such a shop opened and closed. Of course, one's earliest memories of the shops depended on when you were born or first came to the village.

My memories included a bank (Barclay's), which did great business when it was the first to open in Llanishen, as previous residents had had to travel into the centre of Cardiff at one time to attend to their finances.

"That wool shop" (Dalby's, perhaps) doubled as a library, for which you had to pay to hire books, all of which seemed to have titles such as 'Death at Dry Gulch' or 'Passion in the Dust.' It occupied a full double-fronted store, whereas what one would think of as the more important store, Mr. Phillips,' the butcher / grocer / greengrocer, shared the same size shop, split into two, with a baker.

In Station Road there was also a sweet shop, which I eschewed largely at the time, preferring to save my money and my teeth. However, I have since started (in very late middle age) to appreciate more the qualities of sports mixtures, Blackjacks, Spangles, sherbet-filled flying saucers, Jupp's Kimberley Coconuts, and the more sophisticated chocolate confections of Tiffin, Old Jamaica, and those curious Dairy Box-type chocolates all stuck together in a slab of chocolate. Oh, and there was a sweet shop around the corner in Fidlas Road that sold Stothart's Lemonade Tablets. You were supposed to put them into water to create a semblance of lemonade, but I ate the tablets neat, which created the sensation of someone drilling into your tongue with a feather duster.

There was Mr. Livsey the chemist. I remember being asked to go up and collect a prescription for my father, and suffering the indignity of going to the counter and saying "Have you left my father's Asilone?"

And there was the Post Office. That was across the lane from where I lived and I was very friendly with the brother and sister who lived there. There was a large sorting office in the garden there, as well as a manned telephone exchange, as, of course, there was no automatic telephone exchange in those days. Although there were many large houses on the hill up to the station, there can't have been many phones. We had our phone in 1919, I assume, and our number was Llanishen 26.

And, of course, there was our filling station, with four petrol pumps and a shop that sold bulbs and batteries and car polish (I remember the price of petrol as being six shillings and eight pence a gallon for some time … I suppose that's about 33p per gallon, or under 8p per litre).

Our family lived in the house behind the shop. The original front room of the house had become the shop itself, but there were still two reception rooms downstairs, as well as a conservatory, a kitchen, and an outside toilet that had become, after my father's addition of two flimsy walls, an inside toilet: it had no windows and no heating, so you never stayed long in there in the winter. Upstairs, there had originally been three large bedrooms. My parents had the largest bedroom, and, as I was an only child, I had the second-largest. However, as was common in those days, the third bedroom was converted into a much smaller bedroom and a bathroom. This third bedroom was reached through the unlockable bathroom, which led to problems when my cousin was staying with us in the school holidays (her parents being migratory).

My bedroom was quite large, and the window looked out onto the trees lining the back lane behind our long garden. In the lighter summer evenings, I used to lie in bed and watch the upper branches moving and changing with the wind, weaving momentary images of witches and other fabled creatures.

But the thing that held the most interest for me was up the small lane that ran between our house and the post office. It led to a large yard at the rear of our house, which we held on a long lease. The main run of the lane turned at right angles to the left at the end of our garden, then ran up behind the houses in Station Road, and then turned through ninety degrees to the right, and followed the bottoms of the gardens of the houses in Fidlas Road. At one time, we operated cars out of one of the garages here. The lane still exists as of 2017.

If one ignored the unsubtle blandishments of this lane and continued straight on (past a wrought-iron gate that was never used and had long ago been reclaimed by the foliage), you would find a large yard full of coaches (and at one time, an ex-army lorry used for delivering paraffin). There were also about five small lock-up garages for cars, and two larger garages which could each house a 41-seater coach. A third and much larger garage was used for maintenance and had space for two or three coaches. There was also an outbuilding and a ramp.

Surrounding this area, mostly at a lower level, was a large area consisting of allotments and an orchard of apple trees. There was a path that led to the lane behind Kimberley Terrace, and a tennis pavilion adjoining a tennis court, which I believe belonged to the local bank, and was usually inhabited by a strangely morose donkey.

As I have written, I was very friendly with the brother and sister who lived in the post office across the lane from our house, and we used to play together in all the rural areas of Llanishen. Towards Caerphilly Mountain, just past the northern housing estate, there were open fields (now obliterated under Thornhill), and a pond that was reputed to be bottomless, after a cow fell into it and was never seen again. Nearby was "The "Whistling Stile," which you could stand upon and yell "Oo hoo," and hear your own voice echo from the hills. There was also the road up toward the big houses in Lisvane, and the old mill, which seemed very romantic. We would play in the ruins there. Nobody worried about Health and Safety.

But our real playground was the yard behind our house. We could climb trees, play on the lorry and the coaches, drive our little pedal-driven cars up to the pavilion, and hide pastries from the bakery there, only to return and find them ant-ridden.

With no Health and Safety rules to worry about (perhaps common sense was more common then), we often fell out of the trees. I remember one occasion when the girl from the post office fell into a bed of nettles. That was so funny!

And then, having done sufficiently well in the 'Eleven Plus,' I went to Cardiff High School (when it was "for Boys") in Newport Road, Cardiff. This involved a bus ride and a long walk along the lane that ran parallel to Newport Road.

It was there that I became a bus spotter.

Ian Allen, having done quite well for himself with his lists of train numbers for spotters to tick, decided he could do the same with buses, as most of the council-run vehicles thankfully also carried numbers. A group in the school became avid bus-spotters, and my parents would often drive us to out-of-way council depots to ask permission for us to wander around and check which vehicles were there. Amazingly, most staff were happy to allow us to wander around unchecked.

The really strange thing was that, whilst being interested in buses (with numbers), I never really realised that we had a whole yard of the things at the back of our house!

OK, so there is a considerable difference between buses and coaches, not that many members of the public would realise. Today's modern standards have muddied the difference a little these days, but basically the differences are the usage (private hire and contract use, as opposed to stage carriage), the luxury (seating, facilities, et cetera), the chassis (buses need a more heavy-duty chassis), and the operator (buses tended to be run by corporations and large national companies, except perhaps in the more rural areas). And buses carry fleet numbers more than small companies.

So I ignored our coaches (except as playthings) until a gentleman called Mr. Glyn Bowen came to our school to give a lecture, and showed a photograph of one of our coaches (RHP 919, a Karrier Reading 14-seater).

After school, I went to University and studied psychology. I had only really gone to university because all my fellow-pupils were doing so, and I didn't want to start looking for a job, only to come up against previous students from my school who had left three years earlier and were armed with a degree. So, I had no idea what I wanted to do in terms of a job. When I went to see the careers advisor and said that, well, I could go into the family coach business for a while, he seized upon this, probably as an easy option for him, and said it was a good idea, so I did.

Chapter 2

A short history of the early years of the company – My grandfather and his "Arkwright" jacket – The shop – Cut-throat competition between petrol sites – The drawbacks of not answering the phone

Before I start on my personal experiences of operating coaches, perhaps a short history of the company up until the time I joined would be a good idea. Much of this is taken from my website (www.robertfalconer.co.uk), where there are a number of photographs of the company's vehicles.

Falconer and Watts was one of the many small British companies that started almost immediately after the First World War.

In 1919, Percy William Watts and Albert Falconer, who had been in the Army together, opened a small taxi business in Llanishen, at that time a small village around four miles to the north of the centre of Cardiff. Cardiff was then flourishing as a major port, and was around this time the world's leading coal port. For some decades, Cardiff had been increasing in size, absorbing many outlying villages including Llanishen, to became Wales' capital in the mid-fifties.

The first premises were shared with Ernie Yapp, in a small lane running parallel to Fidlas Road, but accessed from Station Road, the main road running through Llanishen village. However, very soon, Ernie Yapp decided his main interest was in car sales, and moved to other premises in Fidlas Road, beside the embankment carrying the railway line between Cardiff and Caerphilly.

Soon after the company started, a small shop and petrol filling station was opened in the middle of Llanishen village. This was in Station Road, adjacent to the lane giving access to the taxi garage, and, initially, had only one hand-pump serving petrol.

In 1922, a second-hand Fiat 14-seater coach was purchased from Charlie Hinton, a coach operator based in Cardiff. Because of this and the need for more space for the taxis and wedding cars, it was clear that larger premises were needed.

New premises to the rear of the filling station up a lane off Station Road were leased in the mid-twenties. Some of the buildings there were later erected during the Second World War as "temporary structures" but lasted into the 1970s. There was also plenty of parking space for cars and coaches (and an occasional lorry), and a large exterior electric ramp.

During these early years, many coaches were purchased from local operators such as Charlie Hinton and Cridland's (there was probably little of a dealer network in those days). The first fifteen coaches purchased, from 1922 to 1936, were a mixed bag that included many continental makes: after the Fiat, came three Crossleys, three Berliets, three Reos, two Lancias, a Bean, a Clement-Talbot, and a Leyland.

It was in the mid-twenties that Albert died from pneumonia, and, on March 12 1925, his father, William Graham Falconer, was instrumental in arranging for Albert's brother, Edgar, to move down from London to take over the partnership with Percy Watts. Another of Albert's brothers, Ronald, was made a junior partner around two months later on May 25 1925, but he left the company fairly soon after. Details about the company are very sketchy during these early years, and the reasons for Ronald's departure are particularly obscure.

In 1927, there was a serious fire at the main garage (Graham Falconer, Edgar's son, is sure of the year, as the shock almost brought on his birth prematurely!). This building, at the new site behind Station Road, was wooden, and was totally destroyed by the fire, resulting in the destruction of four cars. This was reported in the Western Mail. A rather poor photograph survives, and this and other photographs can be found in a gallery on my website, www.robertfalconer.co.uk.

Nevertheless, business progressed satisfactorily over the years, and the coach and car fleet increased. One old newspaper advertisement for Falconer & Watts even boasted "any make of car supplied"!

During and after the Second World War, replacement vehicles were always hard to obtain and the coach fleet (as with most fleets at that time) was made up of "whatever one could get one's hands on," and so never really became standardised (despite the presence of several of the almost-ubiquitous Duple-bodied Bedford OB). Two "new" vehicles acquired in 1949 were ex-War Department vehicles re-fitted with coach bodies.

During the fifties, it became easier to obtain new vehicles and a new Bedford OB Duple (FBO 57) was bought in 1950 and new Bedford SBG Duple coaches in 1951 (GBO 319) and 1957 (NKG 507). As more choice became available, the fleet began to be based almost entirely on Bedford Duples, although the smaller vehicles showed more variety: in fact, between 1951 and 1972, all vehicles purchased with more than 14 seats were Bedford Duples, except for one Commer Plaxton.

Graham Falconer, Edgar's son, joined the company after National Service. He was expected to be able to turn his hand to most things, but took particular satisfaction in hand-painting the coaches and always insisted that the fleet was well turned-out.

One of the first liveries for the entire fleet was blue and cream, which was used from very early on until the early forties, when BDL 322 was acquired and its livery of golden brown and light buff was adopted. This livery was very smart and distinguished, but, just before "mixing and matching" colours became generally available, these colours became unobtainable, and so the colour scheme was again changed, this time to green and grey (based loosely on the livery of a coach purchased from Cosy Coaches of Poole): very soon, a large yellow flash (or two) was also incorporated, and this made the livery more eye-catching.

Image and quality were also felt important in other respects: petrol engines were still specified well after most coach operators had accepted the switch to the more economical, but less refined diesel engine.

In the sixties, the coach fleet began to be run down to some degree, even though this was undoubtedly the most financially-important side of the business.

It had upset Graham greatly to see three beautiful Bedford Duple Super Vegas, all in the same livery of golden brown and light buff, sold and replaced by only two similar but newer machines, which were not put into matching liveries for some time.

Upon the death of his father on November 23 1970, Graham took over his half of the partnership, and was finally able to let the coach operating side of the business improve.

It was at that time that other Cardiff coach operators were beginning to present a more up-to-date image, and it was certainly the time to improve the company's image, rather than otherwise. Even though the operating centre of the company was in a northern suburb of Cardiff, there had always been stalwart support from organisations based in the centre of the city, such as the Wales Tourist Board and the Welsh Office, together with many private companies. However, it was not a time to rely wholly on one's reputation.

Gradually the fleet was improved, although it was always of a fairly small size. In the industrial valleys at that time, there were many lucrative contracts during the week, mainly conveying workers to the collieries. There was obviously far less work of this type in Cardiff, and the capital seemed not to be the best place to support large coach fleets. This might seem surprising in view of its tourist industry and the number of people interested in group private hire for leisure purposes, especially at weekends, but it should be remembered that the number of workers' contracts in the areas surrounding Cardiff meant that there were large volumes of vehicles available for hire at weekends at very competitive prices (after all, most of their financial commitments would have been discharged during the week).

Those Cardiff operators who had begun to increase their fleet size invariably found themselves the object of a take-over from what would eventually became the National Bus Company: Forse's (who had an important garage in Kingsway in the very centre of Cardiff) and Cridland's both sold out to Western Welsh. Many other operators ceased operating or went bankrupt.

By the end of the sixties, Falconer and Watts was the only long-established private operator in the Cardiff area.

So, this was the situation with the company when I joined in 1973. Edgar Falconer, Graham's father, had passed away in 1970, and Graham was more or less in sole control of the coaches.

The coach fleet stood at between four and six when I joined. My father was just beginning to improve the fleet. A new 29-seater was bought in that year, but we were terribly disappointed with it, as, even at that time, there were motorways and fast roads all around Cardiff, and the ageing Bedford VAS chassis just could not cope.

We had been loyal to Bedford since the early fifties, and had even stayed with them when they brought out their new coach chassis in response to the Government's new maximum length of eleven metres (around forty feet). Ford had introduced a normal 11-metre coach, but Bedford decided to bring out a twin-steer chassis. I understand that this was so that they could use more of the existing parts they had available, without resorting to new manufacture. However, we did not like the Bedford 11-metre VAL, and so passed on any work for coaches with more than 45 seats to other operators. This obviously cost us dear.

In fact, we bought our first 11-metre coach in 1973. It was a Ford R226, and gradually our whole fleet was standardised on this marque, which we found more able to cope with motorway traffic than the Bedfords, and more reliable.

We also still had cars (with drivers) for hire. Although we had three Austin Westminsters which our coach staff would drive at times, Mr. Watts handled most of this side of the business, but only mainly for "his customers." I remember he had great difficulty in adjusting to decimal coinage, but was forced to retire when the Council brought in new guidelines about private hire cars.

Our customers were used to large saloons, but the new rules insisted on cars no older than three years of age being registered. We could not justify replacing the Westminsters with newer models, and so decided to pull out of that side of the business. The new rules were very strange though. They would not pass a well-maintained and comfortable Austin Westminster, but were perfectly happy to accept even a small BMC 1100 for such work!

I cannot remember whether the wedding cars were still available. We had had three Humbers, two Imperials and one rare Pullman, but one of these had been replaced by an Austin Princess. They were mainly kept at a another garage we used in Kimberley Terrace, alongside a bungalow which we later purchased.

And then there was the shop! My grandfather, Edgar, had ruled the roost there for years. There were four petrol pumps, metal cabinets to dispense oil, an air pump to inflate tyres, and a large tank that held paraffin. Edgar would dispense petrol whilst clad in an almost stereotypical brown overcoat, almost identical to that worn by Ronnie Barker, as Arkwright in 'Open All Hours.' I think he had a reputation of being a bit tight with his money (except when it came to meeting advertising sales reps. and taking out advertising space in publications that nobody ever saw or read).

The shop I found fascinating. There were many things left over from long ago. I remember a cabinet of Holt's car care products, and a packet of a fuel additive sold during wartime and labelled as making "pool petrol like number one" (I think you might have had to have owned a car during the War to understand that).

We also sold small car parts, light bulbs, and all manner of domestic batteries such as the PP9 size (my father would ask old ladies enquiring after batteries if they wanted a big PP or a little PP).

Paraffin was seen as an important side of the business (and may very well have been at one time), and so a small van (although I have a photograph of two of them together) or a huge ex-army lorry were deployed to deliver the stuff. How a profit was made here I do not know.

But the main problem was that the filling station only broke even at the best of times. This was the beginning (even before supermarkets entered into the market) of filling stations selling apparently cut-price petrol. They would advertise their fuel at "4 pence off" or similar, but nobody actually knew what they were paying. As our petrol was cheap enough anyway (my grandfather would often absorb price increases imposed on him by Esso), and we gave quadruple Green Shield Stamps (even to those on account … and even to those on account who paid very late), I believe we were cheaper than, for example, the apparently cheaper site in nearby Fairoak Road. Unless you could advertise that your petrol was "so much off," nobody was interested, and you had to have sold petrol at the higher price previously (there was a way around this, but we weren't devious enough to use this).

But the biggest problem was that the person operating the petrol pumps was also the person manning the phone. So, whilst you were filling someone's car, the phone might very well be ringing in the office, and you had to let it ring until you had finished serving the petrol.

So, coach hire, definitely the most lucrative side of the business, was being hit because the person answering the phone was often out serving petrol.

Chapter 3

The use and misuse of uniforms and fuel – Traditions and problems with seating capacities – Unwelcome passengers – Giving a bouquet of flowers as a peace offering – Difficulty accessing certain sites – Some of my father's stories – Charity work and its sometimes ineffectual results – Falling foul of the parking rules in Weston-super-Mare

So, when I joined the company, Falconer and Watts was just coming out of the doldrums of the sixties.

My father had taken more control of the coaches, and was at last able to develop more fully what was the most lucrative part of the business.

But, even though I was not employed by the company during those sixties, I still have many memories, mainly pleasant, about that time.

I think most of these reminiscences from now on are going to consist largely of short fragmentary memories … which might very well be more interesting, especially as social history, than a long rambling series of facts about the company

---

There was one man who used to come up to the garages to clean our coaches, purely for the money he got back on the bottles that passengers had left on the coaches. That was until one of our drivers who did not know him told him to clear off … and then that driver (and our others) had to clean the coaches themselves!

We arranged for all our drivers to have smart uniforms, each consisting of a green jacket and grey trousers. The drivers insisted two pairs of trousers would be a necessity.

However, whenever we visited one particular driver at home on one of his days off or saw him when out shopping, he always seemed to be wearing one of these pairs of grey trousers (our sewing badges to the jackets stopped him from wearing his jacket all the time ... or did it?). No wonder they wore out quickly.

One driver's personal transport always seemed to consist of large cars. However, when we finally switched from petrol to diesel coaches, he also changed ... to much smaller, less thirsty cars.

The pumps from which our petrol coaches were filled were just outside the shop, under the almost constant attention of the person in the shop at that time.

My mother once went up to the garage, and surprised this driver with a length of pipe leading from the petrol tank of his coach. He started spluttering and coughing and almost choking. Quite naively, she felt quite sorry for him, not realising what he was up to!

Fuel was also a problem with one of our new coaches, a Bedford Duple 29-seater, this coach being the final reason why we switched from Bedfords to Fords. We had specified that it should have double the normal fuel capacity for long-distance work (not that we found the chassis was up to much of that!). When our driver parked the coach on a side street with a slight camber, he discovered that the way the additional fuel capacity had been achieved was by fitting two normal-sized fuel tanks, with both leading into the same pipe. So, when he parked with the two tanks full, the fuel from one tank flowed down the pipe and into the other tank, which then overflowed and fuel spilled out onto the road. We were not impressed with this arrangement!

We did try both to keep up with modern trends and to retain old traditions. One of the latter was quoting for a 41-seater coach, even though we no longer operated one (the only coach of that size was the ageing Bedford SB from the early 1950s). So, we always made available a quote for a 41-seater (only 50p less than that for a 45-seater on local runs), even though at least a 45-seater would normally be sent. We did occasionally send out a 41-seater though. We purchased a pair of tables mainly for our oldest coach at the time, a 1971 Ford Plaxton 45-seater, which could then be fairly swiftly converted into a 41-seater with the two tables. We also had it reupholstered in our trademark Firth Royd 711 green moquette. One of our oldest customers thanked us for sending her our new coach, even though it was our oldest. The smell of new moquette was very persuasive!

Our of our drivers also had a problem with coach seating capacities reference one customer. We had sent out a 29-seater as she had ordered.

When she got on board she said, "Oh, but I ordered a 29-seater."

The driver smiled, and replied nicely that it was indeed a 29-seater, as she had ordered.

The customer (who clearly knew best, and far better than we and our driving staff) replied, "It is most certainly not. I specifically ordered a 29-seater."

The driver persevered, "Oh, but it is a 29-seater, Madam."

"Of course it isn't," came the reply. "If it were a 29-seater, as it's an odd number, there would be a single seat at the front for me."

The driver finally realised what the customer was getting at. She clearly wanted to sit alone at the front, so that she could lord it over her fellow passengers.

The standard seating layout for the larger coaches is to have a central aisle with a pair of double seats on each side all along the length of the coach, but with five seats across the back (as there would be no aisle there). Nowadays, 3+2 rather than 2+2 seating is commonplace, although there are still five seats across the back.

"Ah," said our driver, "You want to know where the single seat is. It's in the middle at the back."

The customer felt the driver was being impertinent, and did not like this at all.

Regretfully, I have no record of what she said after this, nor do I know whether she made a formal complaint or continued using our coaches.

We also had unwelcome or unwanted passengers at other times.

My father was once driving back to our garage along Lake Road West when he espied a friend waiting at a bus stop. He tooted the horn at him, and stopped just past the bus stop to let him on. He had to get out to check something on the offside of the coach, and, when he returned, he found the whole bus queue sitting on board.

It is debatable whether they were being opportunistic, or whether (as many members of the public cannot) they didn't realise that my father was driving a coach, not a bus. Despite this being illegal, my father felt he had to drive on and drop off his unwanted passengers along the bus route. He didn't charge them, of course. He was careful not to do that again.

When we were in Llanishen, we had our coaches serviced at R. H. Babbage and Son Limited. Their garage was in Kimberley Terrace, and had once been used by the old bus company of Worrell's. They often didn't finish working on one of our coaches until it was almost time to collect passengers. They also had a magnificent black Labrador that the late Dick Babbage had rescued when someone had tried to get rid of it by tying it to the railway lines near Llanishen Station. He was called Toby.

He was much loved at Babbage's, although some mechanics would sometimes clean their oily hands on his black fur.

One day, my father rushed to collect a coach from Babbage's, and then drove off to pick up his passengers. He had driven about two miles, and had reached Lake Road East, when he looked in his inside mirror to see Toby sitting in the middle of the back seat, proud and happy (he loved riding in the coaches). I think my father only just made his appointment, but he had to return to take Toby back home first. After that, he always checked carefully.

I'm not quite sure whether this counts as a welcome or an unwelcome passenger. One of my first jobs when driving for the company was taking a small 12-seater mini-coach to a mediaeval banquet at Caldicot Castle. There, drivers were treated to the same repast as their passengers, albeit "below stairs." I had already formed the opinion that evening work for coach drivers was a bit like having a party every night (although without the alcoholic content). But, one problem with these banquets was that people (mainly women, I have to say) who were not used to alcohol decided they really liked the mead, which was highly alcoholic, although it didn't taste like it. Often therefore they became "unwell" during the return journey. This happened spectacularly on this occasion. The mini-coach was well-appointed for a small vehicle, with a boot, and 12 high-backed seats. But the main thing that appealed to me that night was the fact that it had a large glass partition behind the driver that protected me from any projectiles. I had to change gear by putting my hand into the danger zone, but I made sure I did that quickly and efficiently. The party was highly embarrassed about this, and gave me a massive tip (£7.50 was quite a lot in 1973) … and they even cleaned the vehicle up for me. My father said that, for that money, they could have been ill all over him!

After I had gained my degree from University College Cardiff, I had joined the company to a large extent to try and develop the tours operations. The administration for the company was being handled solely by my parents (with sometimes someone working on the petrol pumps), and, as most of our coaches were available for private hire, there was quite a lot of work involved here. If the fleet had been engaged almost exclusively on contract or bus services (as with many other operators), then there would have been far less administrative work involved, as most days would have been exactly the same, with the same drivers doing the same duties automatically.

And we often had complex private hire tours to plan, sometimes from abroad. We always tried to reply to letters from France in their language, but whether these replies were unintentionally funny, I do not know.

I also drove coaches, as did my father, fitting this in with the administrative duties. And there were other duties …

One particular duty I remember as being distinctly embarrassing.

I'm not sure if it was because of the following incident.

One of our coaches was in our yard, and the drivers insist they were just standing around drinking tea, when the rear window just shattered for no reason at all.

Well, they had each other to back them up, so it was now up to us to get a replacement window.

As the manufacturer of the bodywork (Duple) had offices and workshops in Blackpool and Hendon (London), those were just about the only places from which such windows could be sourced.

So my father phoned up Duple, arranged with a secretary to have such a window left out for collection that evening after the main depot had shut, and myself and a driver, Colin, set off for London.

When we got there, nobody knew anything about the window. Nothing had been left out for us, and so we had to find somewhere to stay the night.

My father played hell with the company in the morning, The apparent culprit, a secretary, was roasted and dragged over the coals by Duple.

My father felt a little comforted ... until he received a phone call from Duple in Blackpool asking when we were coming up for the window.

So, Dad had phoned Duple at Blackpool, and then sent us to London to collect it!

Of course, apologies had to be made. I was told to go and buy an enormous bunch of flowers for the poor girl. I then had to walk, like the famous scene in High Noon, up the centre of a very long office, between rows of avidly watching members of staff, to the secretary's desk (naturally at the far end of the room) to present the bouquet, with our regrets and apologies.

For my pains, I did get a squeal of delight and a kiss, but it was very very embarrassing. Especially at my age.

We then returned with the window duly fitted.

I remember doing one job for, I think, Hy-mac, taking people from Cardiff to Rhymney. I dropped them off, and then parked the Asco Clubman 19-seater coach somewhere unobtrusive, overlooking Rhymney Railway Station. I had to get out to check something, and, on shutting the passenger door, I pressed the lock button. This was the usual way I left the coach ... but only when I had the keys in my pocket.

Then things seemed to start happening in slow motion. As the door started to close, I realised that the keys were in the ignition. I turned to try and stop the door shutting, but to no avail.

And, to make matters worse, it was just as I realised that I was now locked out of my coach with the keys inside that it started snowing. Heavily.

As a last resort, I could of course have telephoned Cardiff, and asked for our one-key-fits-all BX29 that gained access to all our coaches, allowing us to keep the whole set of keys for each particular coach hidden inside.

But perhaps I could get into the coach myself, I thought, perhaps even without breaking a window. The driver's window only slid open a little, but the only thing that held it shut was a little catch that you flipped over to slide the window across. I thumped the window a few times, and was gratified to see the catch flip down, allowing me a little access into the coach. But the aperture was only about twelve-inches square, so there was no way I could squeeze through.

I hunted around and found a suitably long and not too springy branch, which I poked through the window, hoping to hook the keys over the end.

After much time spent on this rather more serious version of toy fishing, I managed to get the keys onto the end of the branch. Thankfully, the keys hadn't been turned in the ignition, and they slid onto the branch easily.

Now, I had to make sure that I didn't let them fall off the end of the branch. Luckily, I managed to extract the keys safely, and opened the door to get into the (comparative) warmth of the interior.

And, boy, did it feel warm!

The lengths of the coaches provided us with problems at times.

Very many decades ago, my father took a relatively short coach (between a 29- and a 41-seater) down a lane and into a field, for some rural event. He had absolutely no problem driving in through the gate.

But it took him a very long time to get the coach out.

Clearly the small front overhang and the long rear overhang created the unfortunate conundrum.

One of the worst places to take a coach, and, unfortunately, a very popular one too, was the Double Diamond Club in Caerphilly.

It was situated off Mill Road in Caerphilly, perhaps in some old railway marshalling yard. It certainly was a railway-intensive area.

But the approach for coaches was horrendous.

The club could only be accessed via one long, narrow tunnel, its cross-section not much larger than that of a standard forty-foot-long coach, and there was a large bend in the centre. Above were (or had been) a large network of railway lines.

One could not attempt to enter the site from the Caerphilly end of the road. One had to drive north to the 'Bowls Inn' in Trecenydd (now partially demolished and replaced by a Tesco Express, as of 2018), and turn towards the town centre from there. On nearing the tunnel into the club, one had to align the coach against the nearside kerb and turn right at just the precise moment to get the whole coach unscathed into the tunnel. If you got it wrong, there was no way one could manoeuvre the coach into the correct position. You had to go out and start all over again. Once inside the tunnel, there was that dreaded bend to negotiate, and then, finally, the bliss of being able to drive into the enormous car park unscathed (if indeed you were). Many drivers often brought their coaches home from venues, rather than kill time there, but, once you were in the Double Diamond Club, you stayed, rather than have to tackle that tunnel more times than necessary.

I'm afraid I have an awful lot of stories about my father. This is not to say that he was the most accident-prone of all our drivers, but just that he was the only one who actually lived with us. He would always tell us of the problems and incidents that had happened to him during each day. And he had a very strange sense of humour that I suppose I have inherited from him (and so, I believe, has my son).

Such as ...

My father was driving one of our cars down Lake Road West, which was always notorious for flooding under the bridge below what is now Eastern Avenue. A little old lady was hoping to get a lift across the waters, so my father offered to help her, and let her climb into the car. Halfway across the flood, the engine spluttered and gave up. Within seconds, the interior was flooded with water, drenching the two occupants. Eventually, the car was towed out. The little old lady opened the door, allowing gallons of water to flood out, and, thoroughly drenched, said "Thank you" nicely, and walked off.

My father once took a religious group to some retreat in rural Gwent. It was an all-night vigil, so he went to sleep on the back seat. Feeling a little cold, he woke up in the early hours of the morning, only to see a long column of candles approaching him down the road, accompanied by chanting. Until he remembered where he was and what his party had come for, he really thought he'd died during the night!

My father once took a party of boy scouts to a camp somewhere in central England, before returning for them a week later. As the scouts seemed to have been eating only beans for the entire week, my father said that, on the return journey, he had to try and avoid all the bumps in the road, or else open all the windows.

On another occasion, he was returning from a few days away with a party (I have a vague memory that it might have been to the Isle of Wight). On the outward journey, he had no problem getting all the luggage into the boot, but, when it was time to return, he had great difficulty in doing so. He assumed that the passengers had been buying a lot of souvenirs whilst away.

But no …

When my father returned to Cardiff and was unloading the boot, a car pulled up alongside, and the driver got out and collected two suitcases from him. He had seen "Cardiff" written on our coach, and was clearly a Cardiffian himself, so he had decided to let my father bring his luggage back for him and free up a little space in his car.

I have to say that I am not sure if the following story is about my father or another driver.

It was very foggy on the driver's return to Cardiff. To make driving easier, the driver decided to follow the red tail-lights of another vehicle ahead, at least as far as the next town.

This worked very well for many miles, until the driver in front suddenly slammed on his brakes. Our coach only just managed to avoid hitting him.

"Why don't you give more notice when you're going to stop suddenly like that?" yelled our driver.

"What, on my own driveway?" came the reply.

Some coach drivers are not the brightest of folk. We had one driver who we told to drive to Cheltenham (which the A40 passes through) and then take the A40 to Gloucester. He got lost. When we asked him why he replied, "But there are two A40s out of Cheltenham!"

It may have been the same driver who took a 40-foot-long coach to one of the golf courses on the outskirts of Cardiff. He drove the party, as instructed, up to the clubhouse, but then found it difficult to turn because of all the parked cars. We eventually had to send out a tow-truck to pull him out of the mud. We then had a bill for a considerable amount of money to returf one of their greens!

I once drove a coach party to Bournemouth, and had to fill up with fuel whilst there. I pulled into a filling station, but the pumps wouldn't work for me. So I went to the cashier and asked why, and was told that our company was not on his list of approved Esso cards. Now we always paid our bills very promptly, so I asked which list he was looking at. It was the list of companies which Esso deemed poor payers (or worse) who should not be served! I explained this, but he would not be moved, so I went elsewhere to fill up. But it has always worried me since that he would only be serving fuel to companies that didn't pay!

As I have written, one place that looked after its drivers was Caldicot Castle, as indeed did almost all places of entertainment. After all, someone bringing up to 53 people to their establishment should be regarded as a someone highly valued. One place that disagreed was the 'Little West' in Southerndown. The first time one of our coaches visited there, the driver stopped the coach outside the entrance, set down his passengers, went to park tidily in their car park, and then returned to find all the doors locked against him. He had to sit out in the cold all evening! Subsequent visits were the same. One customer asked the driver if he had enjoyed his meal. He naturally replied to the contrary. The customer then expressed surprise as she said she had booked for more than had turned up, and, as she had had to pay for the number for which she had booked, she assumed one of the meals paid for would be given to the driver. Not so with the 'Little West.' The Cardiff coach operators banded together, and decided it would only be fair to substantially increase our hire charges there to allow for the driver to return to Bridgend or somewhere else more accommodating. But people liked the place (it was very cheap), and so it still flourished. I believe it is now a retirement home of some sort.

One of our drivers once visited the Cotswolds, and found that our coach was overheating a little. Unwisely, especially considering his experience, he tentatively unscrewed the radiator cap, and boiling water hit his hand. He said he was OK, as indeed he was, and the coach would have been able to have been driven back to Cardiff, but someone on the coach said he had to see a doctor. A medical man was summoned, and he gave our driver some medication that meant he could not drive. So we found we had to send out another driver to bring the coach and party – and driver - back to Cardiff.

We also tried to do our bit in terms of charity work. One of our customers asked if we would be prepared to provide free of charge a coach to take his cyclists to Llandow Race Track (near Cowbridge) to support their charity ride. My father agreed, hoping for some publicity as well. What he didn't know was that it was taking place after midnight. So, not only did he lose sleep, but he also gained zero publicity for his pains.

We had another involvement with Llandow. One of Yeates' dealers asked us and John Crookes of Wenallt Coaches if we would provide transport for a motor race at Llandow. The problem there was that the pits and the starting-point were on opposite sides of the circuit, and so transport was needed to take entrants from one side to the other.

We provided a Bedford J2 19-seater, and Wenallt a 12-seater Austin minibus, and we had great fun. When transferring entrants, John and I raced around the circuit (well, that was what it was built for), and I won! Or so I remember …

These events require a doctor to be in attendance, for obvious reasons. On this occasion, one could not be found, and so, because I had a degree in psychology, they asked if I could take on the role! Perhaps they thought I could use my powers to convince anyone who had been injured that their legs were not in fact on the other side of the wall.   Thankfully, they eventually found someone more suitable.

I think I will have to end this chapter on a less happy note.

Two of our drivers took a party to Weston-super-Mare, and parked in the usual coach park there.   Previously, there had been an attendant to take their money, but now there was only a automatic machine, that expected the £3.00 parking fee to be paid in cash. As this was the first time they had encountered this, the drivers did not have the cash ready, and so they parked up and went to the adjoining café to get change.   To justify this, they also bought a coffee each. When they returned, they found parking tickets on both their coaches.

We received letters from Woodspring Council saying that we would have to pay their exorbitant fines for this. We protested to no avail, and it eventually went to court.

My parents had to go all the way over to Weston-super-Mare to attend court, and the outcome was, in our opinion, a win for us. We were found technically guilty, but we were fined, I believe, a penny. Woodspring had to pay their own costs.

It's certainly an odd way to thank two drivers for bringing up to 106 people to spend money in their resort!

Chapter 4

Private hire to the Continent – "Prestige" work for the Wales Tourist Board, the Welsh Office, Cardiff University, and other official bodies – The Top Ten American Industrialists visit Cardiff – The Pope's visit – Airport work

As we were now, in the seventies, buying a new coach a year, we started undertaking foreign private hire.

We sent our coaches to Amsterdam (even the little 25-seater Ford Moseley we bought new in 1977), Paris, and, for one particular private customer, even Ravenna on the Adriatic Coast, and a number of visits to Kitzbuhel (for the famous Oberammergau Passion Play in 1980).

It was unfortunately that we were never fully reimbursed for many of these latter tours!

We found foreign laws often quite confusing.

When my father drove the 25-seater Ford Moseley we bought new in 1977 to Amsterdam, he parked somewhere which, naturally, he felt was safe and legal.

The Amsterdam Police thought otherwise.

In Britain, a foreign coach found parked incorrectly would probably have been ignored, or issued with a parking ticket which the authorities would have had little hope of being paid. Not so in Amsterdam. The coach, albeit a fairly small one, was efficiently collected and parked in a pound, awaiting the inevitable payment.

On another occasion, I think in Belgium, one of our 10-metre coaches was hired for a party staying at an hotel in the middle of town. The manager at the hotel indicated a kerbside street parking area, and said that that would be accepted by everyone as his parking space for the duration of the week. He used that space, left for him by other drivers, all week, without problem. It was right across a pedestrian crossing!

We were always proud to do what I would term "prestige" work for important customers, as this was good publicity.

We undertook work for the Wales Tourist Board, the Welsh Office, Cardiff University, and many international companies.

I remember collecting a party of French travel agents for a tour around South Wales. The gentleman from the Wales Tourist Board spoke French reasonably well (although I remember a long, awkward pause whilst he tried to remember the French word for 'City Hall,' with me repeating "Mairie" over and over again in my mind). But the English Tourist Board lady who accompanied them, although I admit I believe she was asked to join the group at the last minute, spoke not a word of French. In frustration when one female travel agent declined to take part in the pony-trekking and elected to stay on the coach with me and the ETB lady, I asked if she fancied a walk, and we went for a promenade around the lanes. My conversation, as I remember, consisted to a large extent of "Voici un lapin."

Since marrying a French girl, my French has, I hope, improved greatly.

Another enjoyable jaunt I had with the Wales Tourist Board was taking a group of foreign travel agents through Mid Wales. It had been arranged that our visit to Hay-on-Wye should coincide with the town's "Declaration of Independence" on April the first 1977 (note the day!). Richard Booth, who owned Hay Castle, declared himself King Richard Coeur de Livre. We had a great time there and got to meet King Richard, whose passion for the town and books in general resulted in Hay's becoming the world's largest second-hand and antiquarian book centre. Unfortunately, the stuffy local council declared that they would have no involvement in this and would not recognise King Richard's sovereignty!

I remember one job for, I think, the Welsh Office, that totally stunned me at the time. We were visiting the vast Pumped Storage Scheme at Llanberis, now called 'The Electric Mountain' (it was officially opened by Prince Charles in 1984). I was actually able to drive my full-size coach down a long tunnel for, it seemed, miles underground, and then finally into a vast cathedral-sized cavern inside. It was even more impressive than being able to drive full-size coaches underneath the Cardiff Arms Park. I went on a tour subsequently, but the tour was much shorter, and was not as impressive.

For Thomas Cook one year, we collected the team and supporters for France's annual Six Nations rugby match in Cardiff ... or it may only have been Five Nations then. All went well, until we collected the supporters from Cardiff Castle and took them to St. Fagan's Folk Museum (as I believe it was then known), where the Police were waiting to meet us, and ordered us to take everyone straight to the Airport as many things had been taken from the Castle (mugs, plates, et cetera).

We once provided a shuttle service from Cardiff Central Station to some of the University buildings for my old Psychology Department. I undertook some of these journeys myself, although I neglected to tell anyone that I had gained a degree in Psychology from Cardiff in case that reflected badly on the department's status. One psychology professor obviously thought he had a way with talking to coach drivers and workmen, et cetera, and said that he had heard that

Cardiff had a good football team. At that time we certainly didn't, not that I knew very much about it, but I deigned to reply.

I also took a small party for the psychology department to one of their properties in Mid Wales, called Gregynog, near Newtown. It is a splendid building that looks very much like all the other Tudor buildings in the area ... except that it had been built in the mid-1800s, and was actually made of decorated concrete.

This time, I did tell them of my education, and was probably the only coach driver to take them there who requested to and was allowed to sit in on the lectures.

Probably the most prestigious job we ever did was when we were asked to take the top ten American industrialists on a tour of South Wales.

We were even asked to provide a second, unused, coach to follow the first in case there were any problems with this first coach.

How they would have felt if this second coach had broken down I do not know.

We were asked by the C.I.A. to change our route past Merthyr Tydfil to avoid passing a camp site inhabited by itinerants. They were being really careful!

A banquet was to be provided in Cardiff Castle. Because of the security involved, we were asked to take our full-sized 11-metre coach through the main gateway facing the top of High Street.

Narrow coaches of this size are occasionally built, for instance, for use in the Channel Islands and the lanes of Devon, but only full-width coaches were available in Cardiff.

We knew there was not enough space, but we were told to drive in anyway, and the Americans would pay for any damage to our coach and to the Castle. William Burges would have been turning over in his grave.

So we did drive into the Castle. I bet the driver thoroughly enjoyed it.

And, yes, there was a long scrape down the side of the coach, where the door handle of the gateway had damaged the panels of the coach. But, true to their word, they paid us for this!

Nowadays, much of Cardiff is open twenty-four hours a day. Certainly many supermarkets are, but at one time the only way to get, for instance, a breakfast at three in the morning was to drive along the M4 across the Severn Bridge to Aust Service Area on the other side.

But this was not so when the Pope, John Paul II, visited Cardiff on June the second 1982. Pubs and restaurants stayed open all night. And there seemed to be an almost continental air in the city centre.

We first heard of it when one of our church groups requested a coach to go and see the Pope give his address in Pontcanna Fields. We provided our usual local rate.

Perhaps I should explain what this entailed. For journeys within Cardiff, in normal hours (that is, not very early or late), we would supply a fixed rate. This would assume that the coach would make the outward journey from a single pick-up point, and then be available for hire for other work, before undertaking the return journey to the same single pick-up point.

So this was the rate that we quoted. It would have been around £15.00 at the time for a large coach, I suppose.

It was when we received our second enquiry, and more details were becoming available, that we realised that our coach would be required to collect its passengers around 0500 or 0600 in the morning, park in Pontcanna Fields and be required to stay there for most of the day, before returning in the late afternoon or early evening.   We naturally increased our charges for subsequent bookings to cover this.

We hated having to increase our charges once the coach had been booked (unless the conditions relating to the booking changed). This was especially difficult when we were faced (as were all companies involved in road transport) with massive increases in fuel costs in, I think, the 1970s. But I think we only ever asked a customer for an increase on one occasion (when the booking had been made far in advance).   We certainty didn't ask the first church group who booked our coach for the increase we should have done.

So the first coach that we hired out that day was charged at an impossibly-low rate. I just hope our customers never compared prices …

My father once drove a party of local dignitaries to view the road arrangements on a new motorway around Cardiff.

As it was not yet opened, he was asked to do a u-turn on the motorway.

He loved that!

Whenever we did any of these jobs, we would watch the news on television that evening (we were usually primed by the drivers as to which channel we should watch). It was always rewarding to see our name on the coach that provided the transport, even if it often seemed that the cameras were especially positioned to avoid showing the name!

We also did a lot of airport work.

Cardiff Wales Airport at Rhoose adjoins the Severn Estuary, and usually has better climactic conditions than other airports. We would quite frequently be asked to transfer passengers who had been diverted to Cardiff from there to their destination at a more fog-ridden airport. The situation was so prevalent that we would monitor the weather reports, and put our drivers on standby if we thought it likely that we would be called out.

But sometimes it was Cardiff that was fogbound.

On one occasion we were asked to provide three coaches at short notice to take passengers who were expecting to fly from Cardiff to a London airport as conditions were better there. But, by the time our coaches had reached London, conditions there had worsened too.

We were asked to go to Birmingham Airport, but, on arrival, we were told that that airport was also now fogbound.

The nearest airport that was fog-free was now Cardiff!

So we drove all the way back to Cardiff Airport, where the passengers were finally able to board their planes.

Sometimes air lines would run up large bills with us.

One such was Courtline, who operated out of Luton Airport.

At one stage they owed us around £1,300 (which was a lot in the early 1970s).

We finally received our cheque, thankfully, just a few days before they went bankrupt.

One less prestigious element we later discovered was that one of our drivers, I would hope only if the organiser requested it, would turn up dressed in full cowboy regalia! It makes me cringe just to think of it. In this guise, he called himself Tex. The coach he drove was painted yellow when we bought it, and he used to call it "The Yellow Rose of Texas." He seemed heartbroken when we repainted it into our green and grey livery!

Chapter 5

Day tours – Extended tours – Tours to the Channel Islands

In the forties and fifties, very few members of the public owned or had access to a car.

This was the heyday of the coach tour.

My father said that Forse's, who had a prime position in the centre of Cardiff (near where the Hilton now stands in Kingsway – as of 2018), only had to put out a board advertising an afternoon tour in the morning for it to be full by lunchtime.

By the sixties, after many firms had been swallowed up by Western Welsh, Falconer and Watts was the only private coach company still licensed to operated tours and excursions from Cardiff (although there was G&H Coaches in Pentyrch, whose licences we later bought).

As we felt that these licences could be a great asset, something not to be ignored, we tried to regenerate these day tours in the 1970s. We had two picking-up points in Station Road, Llanishen (later around the corner in Heol Hir, so as not to cause congestion in the village), and Museum Avenue, in Cardiff's Civic Centre.

We had brought these up to date by adding "the motorway clause," which meant that, when a new motorway was opened, our tours (which had very specific routes attached) could use these motorways without a change being applied for. Such changes (or new tours) had to be presented at a Traffic Court, which was very much like a real court of law, with a presiding chairman and perhaps solicitors, and evidence to be presented.

But it seemed nothing could be done to increase interest in these day tours, even after we had added Newport Bus Station (on extended tours), and had bought the licences of G&H Coaches of Pentyrch, giving us pick-up points in Glan-y-Llyn, Morganstown, Nantgarw, Pentyrch, Taff's Well, and Tongwynlais.

We hated cancelling tours because of insufficient bookings.

On one occasion, we had only three people booked on a day tour to Brecon. As we didn't want to cancel it, we decided to have a day out ourselves, and filled part of the coach (we used a 19-seater) with friends and family. One of the three who had paid said he was sad to see so few people booked onto the tour. If only he had known there were only his three paying!

On another occasion, we had a fairly full small coach for a day trip to Bristol. When we came to return, we found that one of the more elderly passengers was missing. We waited for about thirty minutes, and then gave up. When we reached Cardiff, we phoned her family up to check that she was all right … and found that she had got tired and returned by train!

But our extended tours were far more successful.

Amongst others, I particularly remember a tour we ran for two nights at the Hotel Julius Caesar in London. The price was very reasonable, but one night was little rowdy with, I think, a stag night being held there. In the morning, the indoor pool was full of chairs that had been thrown there. One passenger complained to the staff that her husband had tried to swim there, and could have been injured because of the chairs.

"But didn't he see the chairs were in there?" she was asked.

"Oh no," she replied, "He couldn't because of all the sandwiches floating on the surface."

Because of our good relationship with Sealink (who had offices in Cardiff), we were approached by them in 1976 and asked if we would like to offer extended tours to Jersey and Guernsey as partners in their 'Bonus Breakaway' holidays. There were two other respected coach operators involved, R. I. Davies of Tredegar (later taken over by Hill's of Tredegar, and Warners of Tewkesbury, both now defunct), and Jenkins of Skewen (later absorbed by the Shearing Group).

We agreed, partly because they were such good value. The price included return coach travel from Cardiff to Weymouth or Portsmouth, half-board hotel accommodation, coach transfers, and a coach tour of the island (with lunch), plus the "bonus" of a litre bottle of spirits and 200 cigarettes (although this was later modified). Each coach tour was accompanied by a member of the Falconer family to ensure that everything went smoothly (because only coaches of a limited size were allowed on the Channel Islands, Falconer and Watts' coach had to leave the passengers at Weymouth or Portsmouth, and a local coach would meet them on the island).

These became a tremendous success, both financially and in terms of loadings.

As an example, a second campaign, similar but specifically using the Jersey Holiday Village, was run with Sealink in early 1977 – the price of £39.50 included all the above features, including the "bonus."

Keeping passengers happy even extended to my driving from Cardiff to Weymouth by car to reunite some passengers with their luggage.

We were in the office, when someone called in with two suitcases that two of our passengers had left inside a doorway in Llanishen in their rush to get the front seats on the coach. It was a good thing that we provided passengers with our marked luggage labels, otherwise they might not have been brought to us so quickly. I drove as fast as I could to arrive just as the passengers were disembarking from the coach on Weymouth Quay, and handed over their luggage. It wasn't our fault, but they just accepted the luggage, and I don't even remember receiving thanks.

An Excursions and Tours Licence was required to run these extended tours (including an additional pick-up point in Newport, in the lay-by at the entrance to the bus station), and these were granted despite objections from other operators, including one from S.A. Bebb in respect of future applications!

These tours were run from 1976 to 1981, to both Guernsey and Jersey, and rarely had other than full loads.

Chapter 6

Coach dealers' shows – Travel trade conferences and weekends away – The Brighton Coach Rally

So, when I joined the company, Falconer and Watts was just beginning to improve its image. The coach fleet was being modernised, and we were still busy with mainly private hire work (and usually one school contract) for between four and six coaches.

So how did we enjoy ourselves when not working?

Did we engage in busman's holidays?

Well, there were three sorts of junkets we could look forward to each year.

One was the dealers' shows.

Each operator often bought his new or second-hand coaches from one coach dealer. The main ones were ex-operator Don Everall in Wolverhampton; Alf Moseley in Loughborough (and a few other depots around the country, including Cinderford); and ex-coachbuilder W.S. Yeates, also in Loughborough. Why Loughborough attracted so much in the way of coach activity I do not know (one dealer said that the reason was that Loughborough was at the exact centre of the United Kingdom), but at least two major coachbuilders were or had once been based there. We normally bought from Yeates, but were invited to almost all the dealers' shows, where you could look at the latest models, enjoy a buffet and a few drinks, and chat with other operators.

In 1976, our latest coach, a new 10-metre Ford with a 45-seat Duple Dominant I body, was exhibited inside the main marquee at Yeates' (which was quite a coup, as our previous year's purchase had only been exhibited in their yard).

But these show were each for one day only.

Far more interesting were the workshops laid on by tourist boards and ferry companies. These almost always involved a hotel stay and a coach tour of the area, and lasted up to three nights away.

Unfortunately, I cannot comment much on these, as my parents usually snaffled them first. But I did go on one with my mother as joint representatives of the company, and, yes, they were a lot of fun.

And I did go with my father and some other operators on a trip to the Van Hool factory in Belgium, which was very interesting.

There were also day visits to tourist attractions, for instance, Dodington House. I remember these very clearly, as the aristocratic owner of the stately home insisted on talking to the assembled coach operators, and usually told at least one rude joke and had to be cautioned by their P.R. company each year!

But the highlight of the year was the annual Coach Rally at Brighton.

We usually booked at the Neville House Hotel on the seafront for two nights. There were usually four of us, my parents, myself, and whoever was driving.

But it did involve a lot of work.

On the first day, there was a road rally, when you had to drive around the Sussex countryside at a suitably appropriate speed. Then there were driving tests on the promenade at Brighton, reversing a huge coach against the clock into little garage areas marked out by traffic cones, and other similar driving tasks. To see drivers thundering their new coaches along the esplanade, and slamming on the brakes, before, probably, driving over plastic cones to the detriment of sparkling new paintwork could be a daunting sight to a coach operator (but no doubt the other members of the public enjoyed it tremendously).

On the second day was the concours d'elegance. Since the previous day's driving tests, all the crews had been buffing and polishing their coaches inside and out in readiness for this. Some had even painted their engines! Most of the coaches were only days old, but there were occasional vintage models on display, and other operators showed their best coach even if it was quite antiquated. One ancient driver had entered a coach that was around fourteen years old. He even had a ciné camera mounted on the dashboard … and that was probably worth as much as his coach.

In between was the social event of the weekend, a dance hosted by Ford at one of the swankiest hotels in Brighton. I particularly remember entering a competition before the event, and being told I would collect the prize of a television and a video-recorder at the dance … and we even won something in the raffle.

The first year we entered was in 1977. My father had always been interested in small luxury coaches, as we did work, for instance, for the Wales Tourist Board, in particular showing foreign travel agents around Wales, and we needed to negotiate some rather narrow little roads in North and West Wales. There was very little on the market between 12-seater minivan conversions and the Bedford VAS 29-seater (which, as I have written, we felt inadequate for the 1970s). Plaxton had brought out a very smart little body on the Bedford J2 chassis in the early 1960s, and, because Plaxton was no longer bodying this model, we had toyed with the idea of buying a second-hand Bedford J2 Plaxton and having a brand-new chassis fitted. We actually did buy a suitable coach (349 DMJ, which, coincidentally, had been entered in the 1961 Brighton Coach Rally), but then found out that Bedford was no longer producing the J2.

So we were pleased when Moseley announced that they were going to body the Ford A0609 with rather stylish (for its time) coachwork that they were building themselves (the Caetano series of coaches they were offering was imported from Portugal). We were involved at an early stage with the specification for this coach, and we thought we would have a chance of winning something if we entered the 1977 coach rally.

Alas, Moseley thought that they would have a better chance of catching operators' attention if they entered three, and so they arranged for two hastily-finished coaches to be entered. These were not finished to the same standard as ours (we even had carpeting down the aisle in our coach). We felt they detracted from our entry, and we failed to win anything.

Our entry the following year, a new Ford Plaxton 53-seater, also failed to win a prize, and we missed a trick the following year by not entering our new Ford Duple 53-seater, as this was emblazoned with the legend that this was our Diamond Jubilee Year. That sort of thing goes down well with the judges.

In 1980, a new 11-metre Ford Plaxton was entered, again unsuccessfully, but we had better luck the following year.

John Crookes, of Wenallt Coaches, had shared our yard at one time, and he had achieved good results at the Brighton Coach Rallies with his driving skills. Now, he had sold his coaches to concentrate on haulage, and so he was available to drive for us.

My father had collected our new 11-metre Ford 53-seater directly from bodybuilder Duple in Blackpool on the day before the rally, and had driven down (in heavy snow in April) to Brighton to meet us. On the way, the coach had sustained a bit of damage (due to someone else's poor driving), so we thought that might have finished our chances of a win.

The coach was quite impressive, with more than the usual number of extras. It was one of the first coaches, in our area at least, to have double-glazing.

Thanks to John's driving skills (and our fevered polishing) we won the 1981 Welsh Cup.

But, even when one didn't win, Brighton was a great weekend!

Chapter 7

In which we consider other Cardiff coach operators, mostly anonymously!

So, whilst we were the only private coach operators in Cardiff with Excursions and Tours Licences, we most certainly weren't the only independent coach operators.

As I have said, at that time, there was only a small amount of work for operators in Cardiff. There were hardly any contracts other than school contracts, and even the school contracts were few, as there was not the need, as in rural areas, to collect children from a large country catchment area. And the few other contracts were usually handled by the Council's own bus services. We undertook a lot of the private hire work for the government organisations and local companies, as well as for much-valued private organisers, but the days of the street party get-togethers were now almost non-existent. As the number of street parties declined, there was an increase in work for office parties … which was fine, until the party returned to Cardiff, and the poor driver had to take his passengers all around every part of Cardiff!

Either way, if this private hire work took place at the weekends, then there were hundreds of coaches in the Valleys whose upkeep had already been paid for by the National Coal Board contracts during the week, and which could therefore be hired out at cheap rates.

Around this time we usually had four large coaches and one smaller one (say, a 25-seater) available exclusively for private hire work, plus one coach on a school contract. This was certainly far more, on weekdays at least, than any other private Cardiff coach operator.

Quite how we supported our fleet with this arrangement I am not too sure, but reputation played a large part.

For us, providing a decent service to the public was the most important element of our business, and profits came second.

And we always believed in consolidation. So many other operators would find they had a bit of cash over, and so would spend it on their personal cars or a holiday, without thinking of keeping it for possible future shortfalls.

And so who were these other operators? (incidentally, I believe that all these stories are true - I was actually involved in many of them - but do hope they're not apocryphal).

Let's start with one operator who used to work for us as a driver, and I think was a bit of a rogue even then. We had a school contract that involved a very tight right turn at a country crossroads under what is now Pentwyn. The council asked us to increase the size of the coach to a 41-seater, but we said we couldn't, as the turn was too tight. Our driver then purchased a 41-seater himself and took over the contract. But he was welcome to it. I just hope he didn't damage too many panels.

I believe he later went bankrupt three times, each time with different members of his family as "directors." There was a rumour that at one time he even had his dog down as a director! On at least one occasion, he caused the failure of a local fuel company to whom he owed money … they didn't survive, but he bounced back. He grew to some size and his coaches were always quite eye-catching. He even bought new coaches just before we were beginning to be able to compete in that regard. But he soon went down for that third time. Perhaps he would still be operating now if only he had learnt to consolidate when things were going well.

There was another well-known, and this time long-established, operator in, shall we say, southern Cardiff. He had a reputation for running coaches that were rather antiquated and unloved. But he was a character (as were many operators in Cardiff at this time). He later handed over the business to a friend and spouse. We had a phone call from them once. It went like this.

"Hello, you had a broken side window recently, and you sent your coach up to Blackpool to have a new one fitted, didn't you?"

We said yes.

"So, can we borrow the cardboard or whatever you used?"

We were totally unable to understand what was meant.

"Well, when you sent the coach up to Blackpool, didn't you cover up the window with something? Cardboard perhaps?"

We said no. We had sent the coach up without covering up the hole.

The other operator was aghast.

"But what about the passengers?"

We then realised that they were intending to send the coach up to Blackpool, and, as, coincidentally, they had a party going there that weekend (it may very well have been at the time of the Illuminations), they wanted to send it up with a full load of passengers.

We had sent ours up and back empty. We certainly wouldn't have chanced inconveniencing the passengers with a boarded-up window.

Maybe we were too respectable!

Then there was an operator based in the Grangetown area. Despite the fact that we had been operating since 1919, this operator was sometimes described as Cardiff's oldest by the owner's daughter, as we were the longest-established operator, but her father was older than my father!

There are plenty of stories about him.

For instance, he once received a phone call to say one of his coaches had broken down near Bath, and so he drove out a replacement coach himself (with his daughter on board). Near the Severn Bridge, she exclaimed that she had seen their coach heading back to Cardiff, and so the pair assumed the driver had got the coach going again. When he returned to his office, he was surprised to find the driver on the phone asking where the replacement coach was. It had been another coach they'd spotted.

He was one of the first people we knew to have an answer-phone (we always ensured that there was someone on our usual phone, or on an emergency number, whenever our coaches were out). My father once phoned him up, and, finding himself connected to the answer-phone, said "OK, what have you done with my wife's knickers!" (well, that was his sense of humour). A few weeks later, they met, and my father asked him if he'd had any strange messages on his answer-phone. Straight-faced, he replied no, and seemed not to know anything about the message. Finally, my father explained what he'd done, only to be told that the operator hadn't listened to his answer-phone for quite a while, and he even admitted that he sometimes found that customers had left a message booking a coach … for a date that had already passed! And, quite possibly, their phone calls to ask where the coach was were also picked up by the answer-phone!

I went with him and a number of other coach operators to Loughborough, to a dealer's show no doubt, and, on the return, he was keen to show off his new car, a second-hand Mercedes-Benz I think. But we were overtaken at some point by a small, classic, but old, British sports car. So he overtook that. Then he was overtaken again.

This went on for some time, the two cars' speeds becoming increasingly dangerous each mile. Finally, our operator had to admit defeat.

"I would have passed him if only I'd had my glasses on," he wailed.

The rest of the journey was thankfully undertaken at a speed more commensurate with his visual abilities.

Another story, although not relevant to coach operation, was that he once returned home one day to find his wife had sold their piano, because nobody ever used it. He was aghast, and rushed off to find the men who had bought it. They realised something was amiss, and so stung him for a far higher price than they'd paid. But he was happy then. All his savings were hidden inside it!

There were a few operators in the western part of Cardiff too. One of them resisted any approaches to joining an association of Cardiff coach operators as he wanted to go it alone.

One day we had a phone call from that company asking us to cover one of his school contracts.

We would normally have said no, but his secretary told us that the operator was dying, and she was clearly at her wits' end trying to find a replacement coach.

We helped out of course … and the operator went on for many, many years!

Getting money out of coach operators was sometimes difficult. One Cardiff operator had run up a rather large bill with us, but he called in and explained that he was having a tough time at the moment, and asked if he could he delay payment until the next month.

We told him we were quite happy to wait another four weeks.

"Thanks," he replied. "Hey, come and have a look at my new Jaguar!"

There is a bridge in Maindy that I suppose has now been buried under the huge Gabalfa Flyover interchange. But it was narrow, and very, very low. I remember driving through it in a car, and driving very slowly whilst looking out of the window to check there was enough headroom! One Cardiff coach operator had a beautiful 1956 AEC Duple that had either been exhibited at the Commercial Motor Show or had been featured in publicity for the manufacturers. One night, the driver of this beautiful coach drove it at high speed through the bridge ... or a third of the way through it at least. I believe the coach was written off. So was the driver (although he was unharmed).

The Cardiff Coach Operators' Association I referred to earlier was eventually set up, largely so that we could exchange information, have an appointed spokesman, and also try to do a little good.

We approached the Cardiff Council to ask if they would like us to provide transport for underprivileged children to take them to Symonds Yat in the Wye Valley, where the local businesses would arrange food and fairground rides.

They agreed and most of the operators supplied one or two coaches.

To our horror, we found that we had been given, not so much underprivileged children, as problem children. Carers were provided but they just relaxed when we got to Symonds Yat, leaving the drivers to try and control the children.

We had complaints about what went on at the fairground there, and we resolved never to try that again!

Chapter 8

In which we are forced out by developers – We move our base to Kimberley Terrace, Llanishen – We have to find new space for our coaches

The lease on the garage area behind our house, that idyllic land of childhood memories, and our operating base for many decades, was coming to an end in the early 1970s, and we knew we would have to find somewhere new to garage the coaches. At that time this was not easy, as the Council seemed to have a policy of only offering industrial units to manufacturers, presumably as these entailed greater employment.

We were preparing just to be slung out, but my mother, Audrey, did some measuring and investigation, and found that the lane outside our house was too narrow for a standard road, and, in order to access our garage, the developers would have to buy our house (which we did own) and use our side garden and perhaps part of the house to increase this width.

So, we had a bargaining stance.

At around the same time, we realised that the house adjoining the land we rented in Kimberley Terrace to store our wedding cars was up for sale (although I have never understood why it was thought we needed the extra space for our wedding cars)

So we bought the bungalow, so at least we had somewhere to live!

It was number 24, mysteriously named 'Baro.' We later renamed it 'The Coach House,' so that people would know that this was where we were based (although we always had other offices attached to our yards). This caused confusion when someone moved into what had once probably been an actual coach house at the rear of another property in Kimberley Terrace, and gave their building the same name.

We weren't quite ready to move in, so we let it for a few months to someone respectable ... but who still nailed up the wallpaper at one point where it was coming down.

The large area behind our house eventually became Llanishen Court (CF14 5PD). Seven large blocks of apartments have been built there, and there are large areas for parking. Coincidentally, my mother later became practice manager at Llanishen Court Surgery.

So we needed to find a yard, and, as I have written, these were quite difficult to find.

Eventually, we co-rented with John Crookes of Wenallt Coaches a yard in the Leckwith Trading Estate where HGV engineers Henry Morgan Limited had parking space they did not need. We also sublet to Graham Lang (trading as Castle Coaches).

Having the yard so far from our house was a little inconvenient, but it suited us for some years, before we moved to the garage and yard in Godfrey Street, opposite Woodley's (off Adam Street, on the space now occupied by Llewellyn House). There was plenty of space here, and there was less of a problem with intruders from Leckwith Moors ... and we had a handy parking place if we wanted to go shopping in Cardiff City Centre.

There was quite a large building with offices there. We rented this from the Council, but we had to make sure that the standard clause that stated that any broken windows would be replaced at our expense did not apply ... as most of them were already broken!

For a while, we sublet space to Carole and Keith Morris, trading as C.K. Coaches. They soon outgrew this though, and moved on.

There was even a night-watchman there. Well, we allowed a tramp to sleep in the yard, although whether he actually frightened anyone off, I do not know.

As a postscript to this chapter, after my father passed away on August 01 2002 and my mother on November 29 2016, the property in Kimberley Terrace, that is number 24 and the yard alongside, became vacant. My mother had always said that, when she passed away, the house would have to be pulled down. I think this was because, in her later years, she didn't want to be bothered or inconvenienced by major works in the house, such as a much-needed damp-course, and probably rewiring. Hence, by the time she passed away, the house was only fit to be demolished. This was finally done in January 2018. The land was apparently earmarked for four four-bedroom houses, each with a drive.

Chapter 9

In which Falconer and Watts is sold

It must have been in 1981 that I realised that I would not be able to run the company on my own, certainly not to the same standards our customers were used to.

My parents were both unwell and incapacitated at the same time, thankfully only temporarily. As I had no siblings nor close relations who could help, I was the only one running things.

I also realised that I would be unlikely to get married and have a family of support workers (!) with all my commitments.

Perhaps if the family had been rich, I might have done, but we had always only taken a small wage from the company, ploughing most of the profits back into the firm (I have to say that this policy was not shared by most coach operators). Indeed, I had only ever asked to be paid the same as the drivers.

The company was certainly financially sound. Our later policy was to buy on four-years' hire purchase a new coach each year, and then pay it off completely before the end of the first year. Perhaps that is not the best way of handling finance, but it suited us. We had control of our coaches, and only ever had any amount outstanding for a short period of time, and that on only one of the coaches.

It was in April 1981 that we took delivery of our most expensive coach, a Ford Duple Dominant IV with the usual extras that we specified (Bristol dome, cassette and public address system, continental courier's seat, decorative curtains, maximum side lockers, et cetera), plus double-glazing. We felt that the considerable extra cost for the double-glazing would be worth it if tourists could see out of our coach even when there was condensation on other coaches' windows. Either way, the coach was fully paid for by the end of the year.

We won the Welsh Cup at Brighton that year, but we also started advertising the company for sale.

It was certainly not an easy decision, one not taken lightly by the family.

Although we had specified wording that was suitably vague (we didn't want to make our decision public too early), it must have been quite obvious which company was up for sale, as there was only one private operator in the Cardiff area with Excursions and Tours Licences.

It was notoriously difficult to sell coach companies at that time. Often small operators had to sell their premises, goodwill, forward bookings, and coaches for less than the total value of the coaches themselves.

But we finally accepted an offer from Warners Fairfax Tours in Tewkesbury.

They had previously taken over part of R. I. Davies of Tredegar ("shared" with Hill's of Tredegar), Glevum Coaches in Gloucester, and Roy Grindle of Cinderford. They had travel agencies in Bristol (where I believe Eddie Neal had started up Fairfax Tours when his employers, the Co-operative travel agency, had decided not to continue), Cheltenham, Ebbw Vale, Gloucester, Monmouth, Stroud, Tewkesbury ... and Cardiff.

Apparently, Charles Warner had always wanted a coach operator in Cardiff, especially as an adjunct to his travel agency in Upper Clifton Street.

It was quite a shock for myself and Audrey to be asked to remain with the company as manager and assistant manager for the coaches and the travel agency.

I took a course at the college in Colchester Avenue under a previous manager of the Thomas Cook travel agency in Cardiff (for whom we had provided coaches at times) to gain my CoTAC (a certificate of competence for travel agents), which I passed.

And an elaborate system of telephone connections had to be set up.

Falconer and Watts always had been a little top-heavy with phone numbers (and this was in the days before mobile phones). At the time, I lived opposite my parents' house in Kimberley Terrace (it's a long story involving my grandmother), so I had an extension from the main company phone number to my house upstairs. As I had my own private number on the phone downstairs, it meant I had two separate numbers in the house ("Sorry, but my downstairs phone is ringing").

Plus, after moving from Station Road, we always had a separate number for the garage.

Now Warners arranged for the main Falconer and Watts phone number to be available in Llanishen (in my house at least, and perhaps also at my parents') *and* in Upper Clifton Street, about four miles away. And, as I also had two phone numbers for the travel agency, plus our garage, I now had five landline numbers in toto.

As a friend in Rotaract (I was President of Cardiff East one year) jokily wrote after I had already written an irreverent profile of him for the Rotaract District 115 Magazine I edited, it was when I realised that I couldn't make my fortune in life just accumulating phone numbers that I had to find a job.

Whilst at Warners, we still ran the coaches under the Falconer and Watts name, and my mother and I accompanied all the tours to the Channel Islands as previously.

And I also won two competitions whilst with Warners, one to Jersey and one to Guernsey. The first one involved a treasure hunt for travel agents, but unfortunately I was paired with someone who had no ability whatsoever with cryptic clues, and so I had to drive and do the competition … unsuccessfully.

One thing I remember was that the alarm in the travel agency once went off in the late evening or early morning. As keyholders, my mother and I were summoned, and we arrived there to find a policeman standing outside. But he insisted on my going into the building first!

However, there were later changes in management policy at Warners. Responsibility for running the coaches was initially transferred to Tewkesbury, and the travel agencies in South Wales were soon closed down.

My mother and I both finished on December 31 1983.

Warners Fairfax coach tours also stopped, and, as far as I know, the last vestige of Warners (apart from the separate car dealerships) was a series of bus services run around Tewkesbury, known as the Boomerang Bus Company, which finished operating in July 2004.

As Falconer and Watts' reputation and tradition had been looked after so carefully by the Falconer family for so long, it is perhaps better that the name should just pass away, rather than be passed into someone else's hands.

Paperback available on Amazon:
https://www.amazon.co.uk/dp/1530449219

Kindle available on Amazon:
http://www.amazon.co.uk/dp/B01E7RP15A

**The Return of Inspector Pirat: His First Book
(published 2015)**

Paperback available on Amazon:
www.amazon.co.uk/dp/1511429461

Kindle available on Amazon:
www.amazon.co.uk/dp/B00UTKEKPM

And, for younger readers …

<u>Joan Malone Alone (published 2016)</u>

Paperback available on Amazon:
<u>https://www.amazon.co.uk/Joan-Malone-Alone-which-France/dp/1532972571</u>

Kindle available on Amazon:
<u>https://www.amazon.co.uk/Joan-Malone-Alone-Rob-Falconer-ebook/dp/B01HSDJO30</u>

Printed in Great Britain
by Amazon